The History of Money

BY DANA MEACHEN RAU

READING CONSULTANT: SUSAN NATIONS, M.ED., AUTHOR/LITERACY COACH/CONSULTANT

WR WEEKLY READER
EARLY LEARNING LIBRARY

Please visit our web site at: www.earlyliteracy.cc
For a free color catalog describing Weekly Reader® Early Learning Library's list
of high-quality books, call 1-877-445-5824 (USA) or 1-800-387-3178 (Canada).
Weekly Reader® Early Learning Library's fax: (414) 336-0164.

Library of Congress Cataloging-in-Publication Data

Rau, Dana Meachen, 1971–
    The history of money / by Dana Meachen Rau.
      p. cm. — (Money and banks)
    Includes bibliographical references and index.
    ISBN 0-8368-4869-1 (lib. bdg.)
    ISBN 0-8368-4876-4 (softcover)
    1. Money—History—Juvenile literature. I. Title. II. Series.
  HG221.5.R37   2005
  332.4'9—dc22
                          2005042886

This edition first published in 2006 by
Weekly Reader® Early Learning Library
A Member of the WRC Media Family of Companies
330 West Olive Street, Suite 100
Milwaukee, WI 53212 USA

Copyright © 2006 by Weekly Reader® Early Learning Library

Editor: Barbara Kiely Miller
Art direction: Tammy West
Cover design and page layout: Dave Kowalski
Picture research: Diane Laska-Swanke

Picture credits: Cover, title, pp. 4, 19 Gregg Andersen; pp. 5, 6, 9, 14, 15 © North Wind Picture
Archives; p. 7 © Nancy Carter/North Wind Picture Archives; p. 8 © McGraw/Getty Images;
pp. 10, 13 Courtesy of American Numismatic Association's Money Museum, Colorado Springs,
Colorado; pp. 11, 17, 18 Diane Laska-Swanke; p. 12 ARS/USDA; p. 16 Courtesy of Foster Swanke

Printed in the United States of America

1 2 3 4 5 6 7 8 9 09 08 07 06 05

Table of Contents

When you buy a book, you give the store clerk money. The clerk gives you the new book. Buying is like trading. **Trading** means giving someone something they need. Then they give you something you need in return.

When you buy something, you must trade money for what you want.

Bartering is another word for trading. Thousands of years ago, people did not use money. People bartered with each other. Bartering helped every person get what he or she needed.

Native Americans and settlers bartered with each other.
They traded animal furs, tools, and clothes.

© North Wind Picture Archives

Think about a fisherman who lived many years ago. What would he need to do his job? He would need a boat. He would need a net.

Fishermen have always needed the right equipment to catch fish.

Another person in the fisherman's village might be a toolmaker. The toolmaker would spend his day collecting wood and vines from trees or stones from the ground. He would make tools from these things. Perhaps he had a large family. They would need food to eat.

© Nancy Carter/North Wind Picture Archives

Long ago, people used stones and rocks as tools. They also used rocks to grind corn.

The fisherman and the toolmaker could barter. The fisherman could give the toolmaker some fish to eat. Then the toolmaker could give the fisherman a net in return. Maybe a boatbuilder lived in the village, too. The fisherman could trade some fish for a boat.

In some places, people still use bags of grain to trade for things they need.

What if everyone in the village made the same thing?
What if no one had the things other people needed?
Bartering caused some problems.

Sometimes, people had to decide if
they wanted what others had to trade.

Native Americans put wampum beads on strings. They used the beads to trade.

Money solved the problems. People decided to use one thing for money that everyone agreed was valuable to their community. Some people used cattle or animal furs. Some used squares of leather. Native Americans used wampum as money. **Wampum** are beads made from clam shells.

People in Africa, Thailand, and China used small seashells as money. The shells fit easily into their pockets. They could carry the shells from village to village.

Small seashells are easy to carry.

11

In Mexico, people bought what they needed with cacao beans. **Cacao** beans are the main ingredient in chocolate.

Cacao beans grow inside the fruit of a cacao tree. People in the past used the beans as money.

People began to travel to new lands. They also moved to new places. Everyone agreed that gold and silver and other rare metals were valuable. People decided to start using metal as money.

This ancient Chinese money was made out of metal.
It was made in the shape of a key or a knife.

People all over the world made coins out of gold, silver, and other metals. They stamped pictures of kings, queens, gods, or animals on them. Some countries had holes in their coins. People there could string the coins together. People in the land now called Turkey made the first coins about two to three thousand years ago.

Ancient Greek coins have pictures of faces and animals on them.

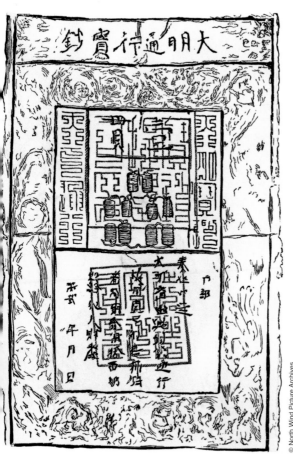

People wanted to keep their coins in a safe place. They left their coins with merchants. A **merchant** is a trader or someone who runs a store. The merchants gave people **receipts**, or written pieces of paper that showed the amounts of money they gave the merchants. People could spend the receipts like money at other stores. These receipts were the first paper money.

© North Wind Picture Archives

This early form of paper money is from China.

15

Chapter ④ MONEY TODAY

Currency looks different all over the world.

Today, people all over the world use different kinds of money. **Currency** is the type of money a country uses.

In the United States, people use dollars. The government makes all the money. Paper money is made in many different dollar amounts. Coins equal parts of one dollar. Pictures of famous Americans from the past are on both paper money and coins.

The currency of the United States is the dollar.

The currency of Canada is the Canadian dollar. In Mexico, people use pesos. Canadian and Mexican money has pictures of famous people from their histories, too. Canadian and Mexican money is very colorful. The paper money is blue, purple, red, green, and brown.

In Canada, the five-dollar bill has a picture of children playing hockey. In Mexico, the fifty pesos bill has a picture of men fishing.

Are you glad that you can use paper money and coins to buy a new book? This kind of money fits in your pocket. It is a lot easier to use than a big bag of grain or a basket of fish!

The kind of money we use today makes shopping easy.

Look at the graph below.
Use it to answer the questions on page 21.

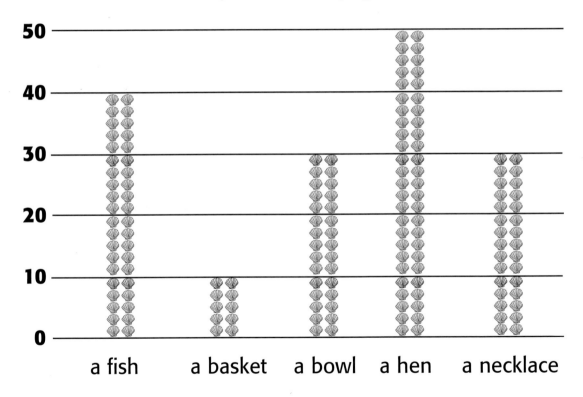

1. Which item costs the most shells to buy?

2. Which item costs the least?

3. Which items could you buy if you had thirty shells?

4. How many different items could you buy with one hundred shells?

Find the answers on page 23.

Glossary

bartering — trading one thing for another without using money

cacao — (kuh KAY oh) a tree that has seeds, or beans, which are used to make chocolate and cocoa

currency — the type of money that is used in a country

merchant — a person who runs a store; someone who buys and sells things

rare — not often found, seen, or happening

receipts — written slips of paper that show how much money has been paid and what has been bought

valuable — worth a lot of money

village — a community of people living together that is smaller than a town

For More Information

Books

Money: A Rich History. Smart About History (series).
   Jon R. Anderson (Grosset and Dunlap)

No Money? No Problem! Social Studies Connects (series).
   Lori Haskens (Kane Press)

The Story of Money. Betsy Maestro (HarperTrophy)

Web Sites

The History of Money
library.thinkquest.org/28718/history.html
A simple time line of money and how it has changed

Money Farm
wttw.com/moneyfarm/lessons/history.html
Read lessons and take quizzes about the history of
money and other interesting money topics.

Math Connection Answers: 1. a hen 2. a basket
3. a bowl or a necklace, or three baskets 4. three

Index

About the Author

Dana Meachen Rau is an author, editor, and illustrator.
She has written more than one hundred books for children,
including nonfiction, early readers, and historical fiction.
She lives with her family in Burlington, Connecticut.